Test #2525
R.L. 6.3
PTS. 0.5

A Tribute to
THE YOUNG AT HEART

MAUD HART LOVELACE

By Ken E. Berg

Published by Abdo & Daughters, 4940 Viking Drive, Suite 622, Edina, Minnesota 55435.

Library bound edition distributed by Rockbottom Books, Pentagon Tower, P.O. Box 36036, Minneapolis, Minnesota 55435.

Printed in the United States.

Cover Photo credit: Ken E. Berg
Interior Photo credits: Ken E. Berg

Edited by Bob Italia

Library of Congress Cataloging-in-Publication Data

Berg, Ken, 1925-
   Maud Hart Lovelace / Ken Berg.
            p.   cm. -- (A Tribute to the Young at Heart)
      ISBN 1-56239-361-8. -- ISBN 1-56239-372-3 (pbk.)
      1. Lovelace, Maud Hart, 1892-1980 -- Juvenile Literature.
      2. Authors, American--20th Century--Biography--Juvenile
      literature. 3. Children's stories--Authorship--Juvenile literature
      4. Minnesota--In literaure--juvenile literature. 5. Minnesotra
      --Biography--juvenile literature. [1. Lovelace, Maud Hart,
      1892-1980. 2. Authors, American.] I. Title. II. Series.
      PS3523.08356Z58   1994
      813'.52--dc20
                                                                    94-3389
                                                                        CIP
                                                                        AC

TABLE OF CONTENTS

"My books are my children," said Maud Hart Lovelace when asked about a possible favorite among her 22. "I love every one of them." —November 1974.

The World of Deep Valley

Deep Valley and The Big Hill are not make-believe. They are a gift from the Ice Age, carved by glaciers perhaps millions of years ago. A huge icecap that had covered much of North America was melting, and runoff water became an awesome river that ripped and gouged the soft soil below. When humans arrived many centuries later, they found a peaceful stream and a winding, fertile, bluffed basin at which to build brave new futures.

Maud Hart's high school graduation portrait, 1910.

For Maud Hart Lovelace, the cozy setting that became Mankato, Minnesota, only 40 years before her birth, would be more than a hillside refuge. It became her world of childhood fantasies and aspiring imagination, filled with the world's best friends.

That's why Deep Valley is fictitious in name only. The characters in the Betsy-Tacy series of books that Mrs. Lovelace was destined to write are inventions, too. But most are likewise based on real people she came to know in childhood.

Childhood

Maud Hart Lovelace was the second daughter of Thomas and Stella (Palmer) Hart, born on April 25, 1892. Her father was a prominent businessman and later an elected county official. Many opportunities came to her and sisters Kathleen and Helen—superior schooling, interesting house guests, theater seats, travel, the freedom to be carefree and to attract endearing, lasting friendships.

The Hart girls' budding appreciation of the arts seemed to direct them toward music, books and libraries. That Maud would become an author and story-teller was clear at age five when she asked her mother how to spell "going down the street."

This surely became Hill Street of the Betsy-Tacy series.

Maud's parents, Thomas and Stella Hart. They were role models for Mr. and Mrs. Ray in the Betsy-Tacy series.

Deep Valley
Comes Alive

Soon Maud was writing stories, poems, and plays on tablets her father brought home from his shoe store. A favorite "writing room" in summer was the crotch of a backyard maple tree. The perch gave her both privacy and a birds-eye view of neighborhood playmates frolicking below. In years to come they would be given imaginary identities in the Betsy-Tacy books—"Tacy," "Tib," and "Winona." Maud herself would appear as Betsy. Events like the opening of the new, grand Carnegie Library would be woven into the stories also.

About Tacy's arrival on Hill Street (Maud in Chapter 1 of the book *Betsy-Tacy*): "… On this March afternoon, a month before Betsy's fifth birthday, they did not know each other, unless Betsy had glimpsed Tacy, without knowing her for Tacy, among the children of assorted sizes moving into the house across the street. Betsy had been kept in because of bad weather, and all day she sat with her nose pasted to the pane. It was exciting beyond words, to have a family with children moving into that house …"

Maud Hart and her friends, who became the characters for the Betsy-Tacy series. Left to right are Mildred Oleson (Irma), Marion Willard (Carney), Constance Davis (Bonnie), older sister Kathleen Hart (Julia), Maud Hart (Betsy), and Eleanor Johnson (Winona of the high school books).

There would be other fancied names for school teachers, classmates, clergymen, librarians and shopkeepers, as very young Maud broadened her world beyond the Big Hill. Her first poem was published when she was 12 in the *Mankato Free Press*. The first short story would be published one year after high school graduation.

The dynamic trio in Mankato (Deep Valley) high school days (right to left):Tib (Marjorie Gerlach), Betsy (Maud Hart) and Tacy (Frances Kenney).

On to the Big City

The Harts insisted their daughters must have a higher quality education. The family moved to Minneapolis in 1911. Maud selected classes in English and romance languages at the University of Minnesota to enrich her writing skills. She became women's editor of the *Minnesota Daily* newspaper and was a frequent contributor to *Minnesota Magazine*. And she was popular in society's whirl of activities.

Maud was a positive person. Yet the busy campus left her strangely unmotivated and unfulfilled. Too much of a perfectionist? Maud tells of the bewilderment in *Betsy and the Great World:* "She wasn't happy, though in spite of her social success, her achievements on the

Daily and the *Mag*, and her name on committees and the membership lists of many organizations. Betsy felt that she had failed herself … She had meant to get an education. And she wasn't doing it … Betsy admitted … that the fault had lain strictly within herself."

In 1914, Thomas Hart wisely packed his daughter off to Europe. Maud had a wonderful time that she would turn into fiction decades later as *Betsy and the Great World*. She returned home at the outbreak of World War I. She would find a husband before too long in her beloved Minnesota.

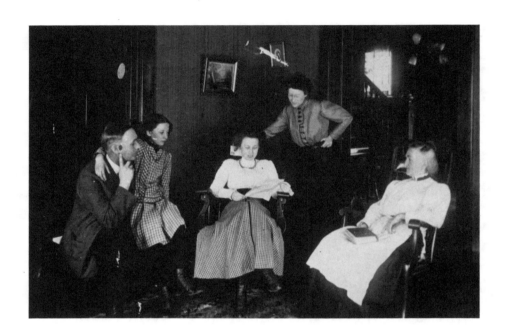

The Hart family gathers in the "Hill Street" living room as Maud (center) reads a letter from older sister Kathleen, studying music in Germany. Father, Thomas Hart, is at left with younger daughter, Helen, on his knee; Maud; mother, Stella Hart; and grandmother, Mrs. C.H. Austin visiting from California. All would have roles in Betsy-Tacy books.

The Job, a Boyfriend

Maud's employer at the Minneapolis publicity firm where she was working in 1917 introduced her to Delos Lovelace. Both were Minnesota-born, had been students at the same university, had a love of writing, engaging personalities, and together "cut a fine figure." It was love at first sight. Maud and Delos were married November 29, 1917, he in his military uniform—six months after they had met.

Now Maud Hart Lovelace, for the first time, had to learn about homemaking. This, she admitted, did not come easily. But she had more opportunity for quietness and creating short stories, and settling into her major professional ambition—authoring significant books.

Maud Hart and Delos Lovelace, shortly before
their marriage in Minneapolis, 1917.

Maud relished history, historical settings, and adult themes. Betsy-Tacy as a children's series was not yet an idea. *Early Candlelight*, her second novel and set on the 1840s frontier, was foremost on her mind and that would take much research. Furthermore, she and Delos were collaborating on a romance theme that would take the title, *Gentlemen From England,* also in a Minnesota setting. Like previous works, both were published, and these received special critical approval. "Delos and I worked well together, despite risking 17 years of happy married life to do it," Maud chuckled. "We succeeded, I suppose, because we never, ever, quarreled."

Army soldiers stationed in St. Paul recognized
Maud on September 27, 1929, thanking her for
Early Candlelight and the nostalgic look at the
first years of old Fort Snelling. They gave a
gala reception and staged a full-scale field
dress review. The St. Paul newspaper said
Maud was the first American woman civilian to
be so honored. She was pictured standing
beside the fort's commandant as troops
marched by. Delos, a World War I veteran, was
impressed.

On to Betsy-Tacy

The 1930s proved to be an exciting decade for Maud and Delos Lovelace. Daughter Merian was born (a son had died at birth earlier) and opportunity came for Delos to make "the big time" in newspapering, in New York City. Merian came something of a surprise since Mrs. Lovelace had been married 13 years. So, now she must be a full-time mother when the Lovelaces were just making their mark as novelists. And there were the pressures of Delos' new position as a headlined newspaper editor on a major metropolitan daily. "At the moment," Maud said, "our child is my main concern."

Fortunately, *Betsy-Tacy* also found life during this hubbub. As Merian grew, Maud began to recite bits of stories from her own girlhood. They were meant to amuse at bedtime. Merian was so delighted with them that they were spun over and over, usually with new twists and additions. This is something Maud could do at home without research, what with her diaries and photographs. Simply put these tales on typing paper and approach her agent, Maud thought. She did. The Thomas Crowell Company accepted the book and that was the beginning of the Betsy-Tacy series.

Betsy-Tacy appeared in 1940. Childhood in Mankato was in full bloom again, this time on printed book paper—the first bashful hellos among the girls, the early capers of Betsy, Tacy, Tib, Winona, and friends.

There would be 10 Betsy-Tacy books in all, following Betsy and her lovable companions through girlhood and high school in Deep Valley, to Betsy's wedding at the far end of Deep Valley—Minneapolis.

Where Betsy and Tacy were born in book form, in 1940—the home of Maud Hart and Delos Lovelace, and daughter Merian, 63 Wyatt Road, Garden City, New York.

"Real" Characters

Many storybook scenes and events parallel Maud's youth, while others are fiction. The cast was based on actual people. Mr. and Mrs. Ray were developed from her parents, Tacy was Frances Kenney. Tib was Marjorie Gerlach, sisters Kathleen and Helen were Julia and Margaret, and handsome Joe, Betsy's high school rival, represented Delos. About her own role, Maud said: "Betsy is like me except that, of course, I glamorized her to make her a proper heroine." Artwork by Lois Lenski and Vera Neville brought this cast of characters to life.

A rare photo of Marjorie
Gerlach (Tib) in her grade
school "dancing dress."

The genuine, warm, readable yarns proved a pleasant surprise to a wide, enthusiastic audience. Maud also wrote three stories about Deep Valley in which Betsy is not the leading character—and five other childrens books.

The Trees Kneel At Christmas, set in Brooklyn but based on a Lebanese community in Mankato when Maud was a girl, arrived in 1951. When the Lovelaces retired to California in 1954, she put finishing touches on *What Cabrillo Found*. *The Valentine Box* marked the end of her writing career in 1966.

Writing did not make Maud and Delos wealthy, but the additional income was welcomed, especially to the young family when in New York. "It made our lives comfortable," Maud said.

Recently, thanks to the hard work of her fans, there has been a revival of Betsy-Tacy interest. The entire series is being reintroduced by Harper-Collins, publishers. *The Trees Kneel At Christmas* is being reissued by Abdo &Daughters Publishing, in cooperation with Merian Lovelace Kirchner. A new generation of young folks will be catching the Betsy-Tacy fever from their parents.

As widows, Maud and her childhood friend, Frances Kenney
Kirch (Tacy), visited the royal palace in Madrid, Spain. They
reinacted scenes from a Betsy-Tacy episode written 30 years
earlier. This was their last real-life adventure together.

Mankato is Still Home

Merian Lovelace Kirchner represented her mother when the new Mankato regional library was opened in 1977. The children's wing, decorated with a large mural of Deep Valley scenes and Betsy-Tacy personalities, is dedicated to Maud and carries her name. The library offers an annual Maud Hart Lovelace Reading Award for children grades 3-8. A map of the "Betsy-Tacy Trail" is given to visitors wishing to tromp the Big Hills and stop to rest on the Maud Hart Lovelace memorial bench. Mankato has hosted a national Betsy-Tacy Society convention.

Maud kept up her friendship with the "real" Tacy and Tib, who had also moved elsewhere, for the rest of their lives.

A wall mural in the Maud Hart Lovelace wing of
the Minnesota Valley Regional Library in
Mankato, Minnesota. It depicts Deep Valley
and Betsy-Tacy characters, as envisioned and
painted by Marian Anderson.

Maud Hart Lovelace, last survivor of the Betsy-Tacy players, died in Claremont California on March 11, 1980, just before her 88th birthday.

At Maud's request, funeral services were held at the Episcopal Church in Mankato. Burial was at Glenwood Cemetery, appropriately on the slope of a wooded and shaded hill in Deep Valley.

… We all like to lose ourselves now and then in the blissful, carefree memories of childhood. Maud Hart Lovelace had a reassuring touch for capturing those precious years for us on the pages of her Betsy-Tacy books. Welcome back to the Big Hill Maud. You never really left...

—"Home on the Hill" testimonial,
Mankato Free Press,
March 14, 1980.

Maud Hart Lovelace's favorite portrait of herself as a writer was taken in 1948, wearing the "finger wave" hairstyle of the time.

BOOKS BY MAUD HART LOVELACE

Betsy-Tacy
Betsy-Tacy and Tib
Betsy and Tacy Go Over the Big Hill
Betsy and Tacy Go Downtown
Heaven to Betsy
Betsy in Spite of Herself
Betsy Was a Junior
Betsy and Joe
Betsy and the Great World
Betsy's Wedding
Carney's House Party
Emily of Deep Valley
Winona's Pony Cart
The Golden Wedge
(With Delos Lovelace)
The Tune is in the Tree
The Trees Kneel at Christmas
What Cabrillo Found
The Valentine Box

ADULT FICTION BY MAUD HART LOVELACE
The Black Angels
Early Candlelight
The Charming Sally
Petticoat Court
One Stayed at Welcome
(With Delos Lovelace)
Gentlemen From England
(With Delos Lovelace)

Grateful acknowledgement and credits to Merian Lovelace Kirchner, Shirley Lieske of the Minnesota Valley Regional Library, Amy Dolnick, Kelly Reuter, Nancy Berg, and Sharla Whalen, who generously shared their informational files and memories of Maud Hart Lovelace on behalf of Betsy-Tacy fans everywhere.

Photographs are through the courtesy of the Blue Earth County Historical Society, Shirley Lieske, Nancy Berg, Merian Lovelace Kirchner, and the author.

For information on the Betsy-Tacy Society write:

Betsy-Tacy Society
Blue Earth County Historical Society
415 Cherry Street
Mankato, Minnesota 56001